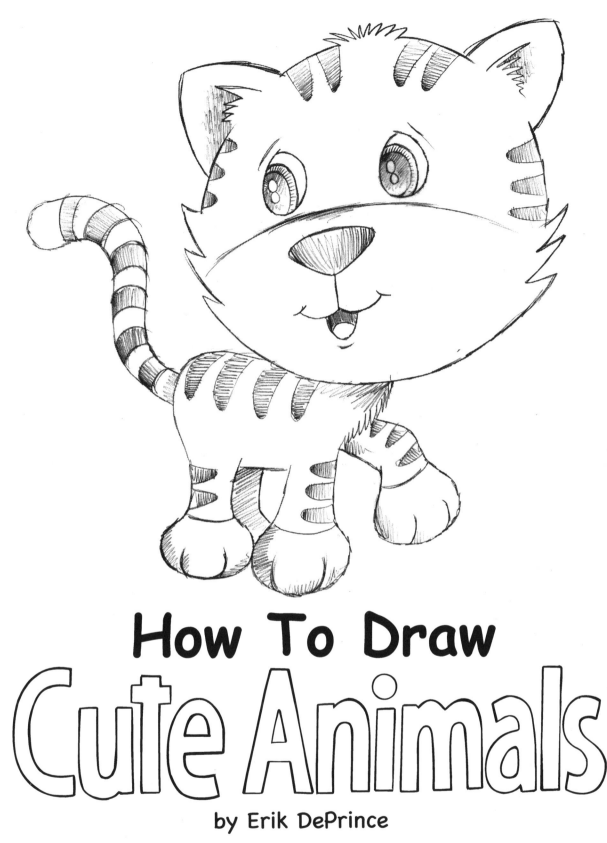

How To Draw
Cute Animals

by Erik DePrince

www.facebook.com/eriksworldofcuteness

P9-CKX-004

Elephant

Whale

Swordfish

Dinosaur

Horse

Goat

Goose

Zebra

Turtle

Tiger

Bull

Pegasus

Dog

Ram

Lion

Alligator

Monkey

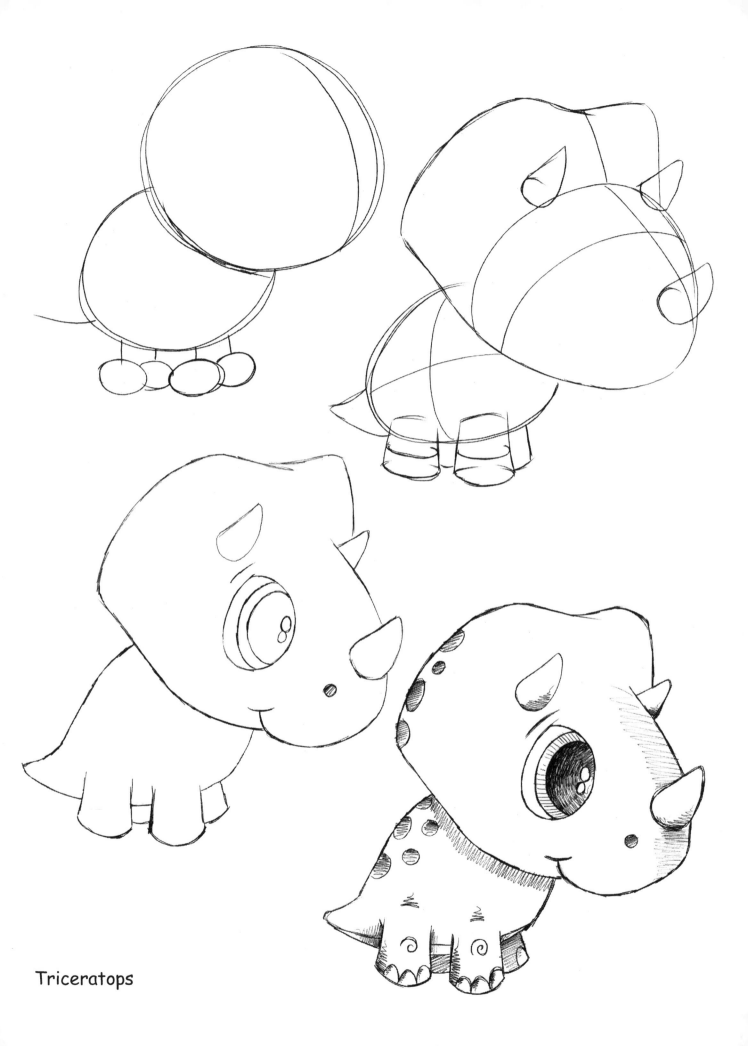

Triceratops

Stegosaurus

Hippopotamus

Tyrannosaurus rex

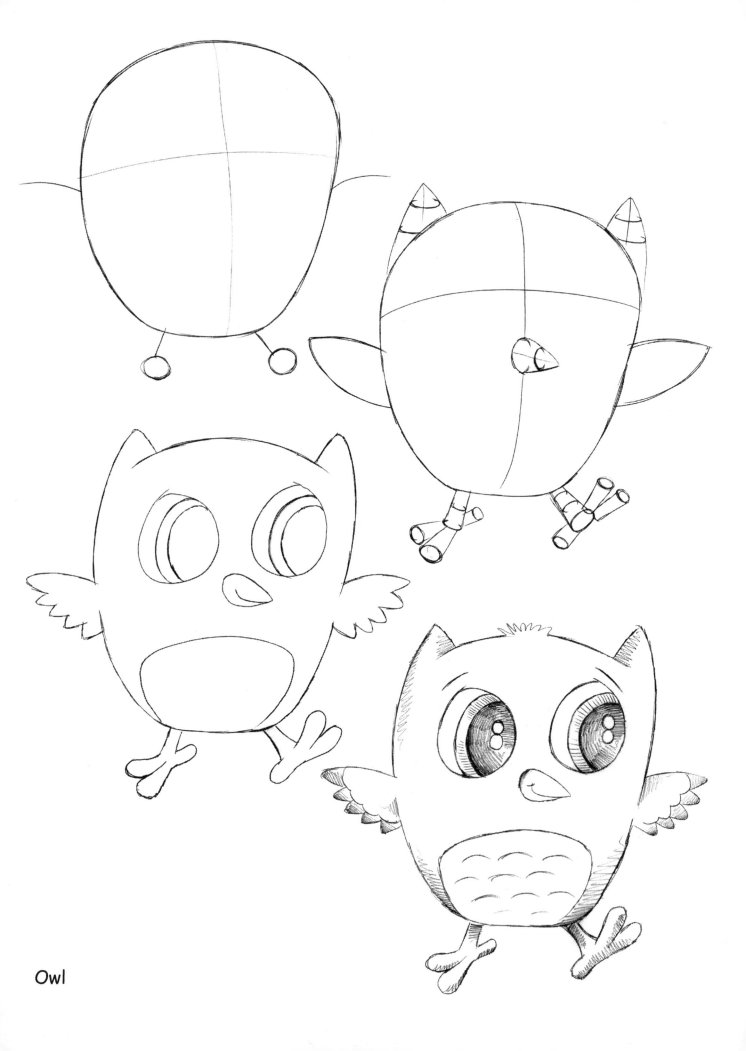

Owl

Elephant

Rhino

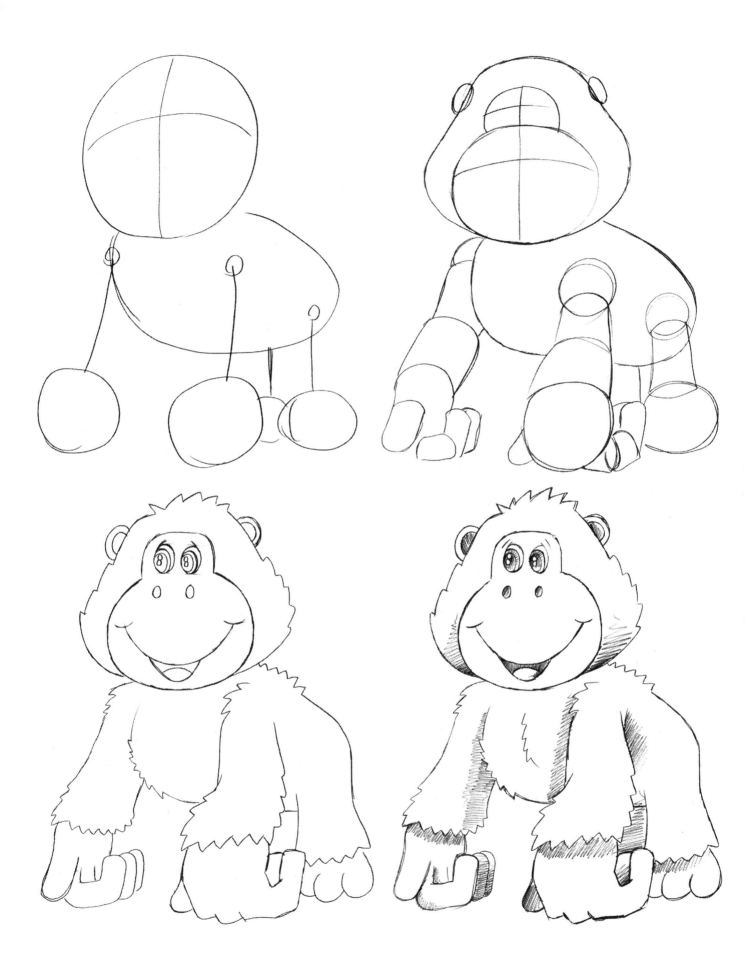

Gorilla

Cow

Toucan

Shark

Duck

Unicorn

93385154R00020

Made in the USA
San Bernardino, CA
08 November 2018